THE LOON BOOK

THE LOON BOOK

by
Thomas Hollatz
with
Corinne A. Dwyer

NORTH STAR PRESS
ST. CLOUD, MINNESOTA

Acknowledgements

A special thanks to Linda Bein, Tim Smalley, the Minnesota and Wisconsin Departments of Natural Resources, Mercer Chamber of Commerce, James LaVigne, Richard Van Order, Jeff Ayers, Woody Hagge, Roger Tory Peterson, Jim Pierce of Wisconsin Project Loon Watch, Tom Klein of the Sigurd Olson Environmental Institute, U.S. Bureau of Sport Fisheries and Wildlife, John McPhee, Sen. William Proxmire, Sen. Rudy Boschwitz, Rep. David Obey, Kathleen White, Mary Herrick and her third graders, Ron Eckstein, the 700 loon-watch volunteers and my first copy chief at the Chicago Tribune, the late James Francis Derby.

This book is dedicated to Judi Lowmiller.

Loon legends drawings by Patrick A. Dwyer.

Second Printing: June 1985

Third Printing: July 1987

ISBN 0-87839-040-5

Table of Contents

Photo: Tom Hollatz.

Introduction

The Loon Lake Ghosts, Antioch, Illinois

Loon Lake and the Villa Rica subdivision is the first wilderness area I ever knew and loved. It was wilderness. It was thick with trees, enclosing two beautiful lakes.

I was born and reared on the great South Side of Chicago and heading "up north" to Loon Lake from Memorial Day to Labor Day was always a treasured time. The trouble was I never wanted to come home. I believe it was then I vowed never to live in a big city but in a place near the heart of the woods. The northwoods of Boulder Junction, Wisconsin fulfills that dream.

But my Illinois Loon Lake still is a special place for me.

I'll not forget the night of my first overnight camping trip. The campers included, in addition to myself at the age of 9 years, my younger brother Dick, and an older friend, Bobby. My mother trusted Bobby because his father was a deputy sheriff or so everyone thought in the Villa Rica subdivision. No one never knew for sure, but old Elmer always looked honest.

1

Mother packed blankets and enough food for a two-week safari. Two six-packs of Double Cola were also added to the box.

Bobby aimed his dad's sleek rowboat powered by a small Evinrude motor toward the mysterious Hidden Channel, located at the northeast corner of the "back lake" or East Loon Lake.

The Hidden Channel was a place about which legends and strange stories were hatched. It always smelled funny—a mud-like aroma. The land area was like dry muck or peat-like. A boggy smell of rotting things.

The land around the channel always looked dead. There were many fallen and rotted trees. There were no homes in the area although an occasional "lot for sale" sign popped out of the gloom. It was the remotest part of the lake—the end of the world to young lads.

Although it was twilight when we pulled the boat on

the shore, we decided to get our fire going. We had no tent but placed old blankets on the ground around our fire.

The sky got darker by the second. As we munched on ham sandwiches our eyes fixed on the fire. Except for the crackling of the flames, all was silent.

Bobby entertained us with some of his most creepy ghost stories. A young boy lost the money his mother had given him to buy meat . . . he got the meat by going to a cemetery and stealing the liver of a newly buried corpse . . . Later that night the corpse came calling at the boy's house seeking to get his liver back! You have the gist of the tale. It ended with Bobby grabbing my throat and screaming "I want my liver. . . ."

It was about then that we heard the first scream of a Common loon. "God, what was that?" Was my reaction. It was eerie and, after ghost stories, blood curdling! The loon screamed again. The sound was so piercing it seemed to go right through us.

Bobby offered that it was some strange boy-eating animal looking for its nightly meal.

The loon echoed again throughout the land of the Back Lake Hidden Channel.

Imaginations ran wild. Maybe it was a laughing crazy man swimming to get us, just like the dead gent with the missing liver.

The scream shook our young bones again.

Bobby doubled-up with laughter. "It's only a loon."

He roared again. "They laugh like crazy people."

I had seen a stuffed loon that my grandfather had at his summer home on Loon Lake. But memory of that "unstuffed" loon sound would haunt me forever. The only bird sounds I had ever noticed before were the soft coos of Chicago pigeons.

It was two in the morning and several loon screams later when we all decided "it looked like rain" although we couldn't see a thing.

We repacked the supply box and doused the fire with lake water. The smoke imbedded itself in our clothing. It was only a half hour later when we returned to our cottage. We knocked on the latched screen door.

My mother called from her upstairs bedroom, "Who's there?" "It's us. It looked like rain." A faint chattery laugh sounded down the lake from Hidden Channel as mom unhooked the screen door.

Despite my eerie introduction to the Common Loon in the Hidden Channel of Loon Lake, the urge to know about the bird became a passion.

Photo credit: Minnesota Department of Natural Resources.

LOON

(Upper figures, Winter plumage; lower figure, breeding plumage)

National Audubon Society

A lonely lake, a lonely shore,
A lone pine leaning on the moon;
All night the water-beating wings
Of a solitary loon.
                              Lew Sarett

The Loon
in Fact

The loon is an ancient bird. Fossils of loon-like diving birds essentially identical to living specimens have dated back to the Paleocene period, some 65 million years ago.

Phylogeny

Loons are diving birds, related to merganzers, cormorants and grebes. A member of the Order *Gaviiformes* and the Family *Gaviidae* (Gay-VEE-ih-dee), there are four representatives on the North American continent. The Arctic Loon (*Gavia arctica*) is nearly circumpolar in habit, nesting on cold tundra lakes and waterways. The Yellow-billed Loon (*Gavia adamsii*) is the largest loon and also is a tundra breeder. The Red-throated Loon (*Gavia stellata*) is the smallest of the four and a coastal breeder of the far north. The Common Loon (*Gavia immer*) ranking second largest in size is the most wide-ranging loon and the only one nesting in the lower forty-eight states, principally Wisconsin, Minnesota and Michigan as well as a few isolated pockets of northern New England. This loon is

7

also found in Canada, Alaska, Greenland, and Iceland. It is with the Common Loon that this book concerns itself.

Description

The Common Loon is a large water bird. Averaging twenty-eight to thirty-six inches from bill to tail, it corresponds with the length of the Canada Goose, although the loon has a shorter neck in relation to body size. The wingspan of the loon is nearly five feet; that of the Canada Goose is five and a half feet. Thus, in this comparison with the more familiar goose, the loon appears to be a longer bodied bird with shorter wingspan. Loons weigh between eight and eleven pounds.

A loon has been described during its artful and quick dives as a powered rock. Indeed, as a diving bird it is superbly adapted to its aquatic life. It is a streamlined torpedo, its total form designed carefully.

The beak of the Common Loon is a strong, evenly-

Note the sharpness of the bill and the tapering of the head. *Photo: Tom Hollatz*

8

With a powerful thrust of its webbed feet, the loon dives under the surface of the lake. Legs placed far back on its tapered body make the loon a superb diver. *Photo credit: Minnesota Department of Natural Resources.*

tapered dagger of approximately four inches. Used to grab its prey during dives, this sharp weapon can also be an effective defense against predators and is sometimes used against rival males during territorial disputes.

Loons have red eyes. Besides being a striking contrast to the greenish black head, the color is an important functional adaptation. This red pigmentation of the retina filters light, improving vision in the darkened realm of the loon's underwater hunting grounds. Loons often hunt at great depths; this aid to vision is very necessary.

The elongated, carefully tapered body of the loon moves through the water with ease, creating less turbulence which slows speed and expends energy. On the surface, the loon carries its neck and head in a graceful curve, fairly close to its body. Underwater, the loon's head is extended toward the prey with just enough crook to the neck to provide the strike-force to grab the fish.

The propelling force in the loon's expert hunting system is its large webbed feet which are placed at the extreme back of the loon's body. The tarsus or shank of each powerful leg is flattened laterally allowing easy movement of the leg in water. The three large front toes are fully webbed and the small hind toe is nearly on the same level. It also has a small flap and is placed laterally to aid in the power of each stroke. The legs work like oars, almost at right angles to the loon's body.

The wings are also used in underwater propulsion so that at times the bird is almost flying through the water. Also, they aid balance and permit lightning fast turns while pursuing prey. The loon is quite a strong and capable flier, but has great difficulty making the transition from the surface of the water to the air. With its legs placed so far back on its body and because it is a large bird, it is necessary for the loon to run across the surface of the water for up to a quarter of a mile before the frantic beating of its wings can lift it aloft. This problem of take-off, and the need for a long runway, requires a minimum size limit of the body of water where a loon may set down. Loons are seldom found in lakes under nine to ten acres in size. Landing is equally difficult for the loon as the feet cannot be brought forward enough to be used effectively as landing skiis as other webbed-footed birds do. Yet they usually manage to glide in with some grace.

The loon's tail is an abbreviated affair. It is short and possesses eighteen to twenty very stiff feathers. The loon uses its tail as a rudder underwater as well as in flight.

Internal Adaptations

Internally, loons are further adapted to their swimming/diving lifestyle. Many of the bones of the loon's body are solid rather than air-filled (pneumatized) as in most birds. This facilitates diving. A loon's specific gravity is closer to that of water than that of a duck which buoyantly floats on the surface. Further, a loon can change its specific

The Great Northern Diver. *Photo credit: Woody Hagge, 1981.*

gravity by expelling air from its body and even from within its feathers. This allows the loon to sink slowly under the surface of the water with scarcely a ripple and permits fast dives.

Like other diving birds, loons undergo changes in their respiratory and circulatory physiology which allows them to remain underwater for fairly long periods. (Though most dives last a minute or less, loons have been timed in dives lasting up to five minutes or longer.) Loon blood is rich in hemoglobin, allowing the bird to retain more oxygen than most birds. Its muscles have large amounts of myoglobin, a respiratory pigment, allowing the storage of large amounts of oxygen for underwater use. ". . . when they dive," wrote William H. Amos in *The Life of the Pond—Our Living World of Nature*, "their heartbeat slows down as does their general metabolism, and only their brains, sensory organs and muscles receive their normal quotas of oxygen. Carbon dioxide accumulates in their system, but is exhaled when the birds reach the surface." Those organs not essential in the procuring of food during the long dives have a high tolerance to reduced oxygenation.

Even the loon's basic color pattern, dark on top and light underneath is adaptive. By having a white belly, a loon is less visible to fish as it swims through the light-filled

Such loon social gatherings occur regularly during late summer. This family reunion took place on Trout Lake in Boulder Junction, Wisconsin. *Photo: Tom Hollatz.*

Standing Loon. Note the wonderful patterning of the white over the back and wings. *Photo credit: Woody Hagge, 1981.*

water above them. During dives, the darker back is a camouflage to an enemy looking down through the water. The feathers form a dense, waterproof envelope around the loon protecting it from the icy northern water. Even a newly hatched chick is well insulated with waterproof down.

Plumage

As is common with most birds, the loon changes its plumage twice annually in the prenuptial and postnuptial molts. The prenuptial molt occurs in late winter before the birds leave their winter feeding grounds. Both the male and the female birds are colored the same. In the Common Loon, this breeding plumage consists of a velvety, dark greenish-black head, dark bill, white belly and dark back liberally splashed with white cross-banding and speckles. The Common Loon has a throat slash and striking neck bands of vertical white stripes. Its red eyes have already been noted. In late summer, on the breeding grounds, the

Winter plumage (background) and the summer plumage (foreground) of the Common Loon. *Photo credit: National Audubon Society.*

loon molts its beautiful plumage and dons a plain, brownish grey back, top of neck and head over a white belly and throat. The beak is also lightened. Again, both sexes are marked the same as are the newly fledged youngsters. During this molt, the flight feathers are retained. The flight feathers are molted once annually on the winter range.

Habitat

The summer range of the Common Loon, though shrinking further northward each year, still includes the upper halves of Michigan, Wisconsin, and Minnesota as well as isolated lakes in upper New England, Canada, Alaska and some areas of Greenland and Iceland. Northern wooded lakes which are of the minimum size of nine to ten acres, some rivers, some lakes of 100 acres or more and bays of still larger lakes become the territory of individual pairs of loons. They are especially fond of lakes with islands which provide nest sites with extra protection from predation and intrusion. And loons are especially sensitive to intrusion. The waters the loon chooses for its summer nesting and hunting grounds need to be secluded because nesting is a difficult time for loons. For this reason, the summer range of the Common Loon has shrunk northward over the years as lake shore is developed, bringing motorboats, too many inquisitive onlookers, destructive family pets and even a greater influx of scavenger-type wildlife such as the raccoon and the skunk which prey on loon eggs.

Male Displays

The male loon arrives on northern lakes soon after the ice goes out. It is believed that they return to the same lakes year after year. At this time there is much yodeling and displaying as younger males without territory try to displace older birds. Two males will face each other and with loud vocalizations and wild flapping of their powerful wings stand up on the water in what has been termed the "penguin-dance." As with most birds the ordering of

Display of fine plumage in an exaggerated stretch. *Photo credit: Minnesota Department of Natural Resources.*

territorial boundaries is handled primarily by ritual but the male birds especially those equal in size can escalate their displays into beak sparring and jabbing. Occasionally, one loon male manages to grasp its rival's neck and forces him under water. But this kind of victory is rare.

Courtship rituals

The females arrive and courtship begins. Though it is believed that loons mate for life these rituals are repeated each year, renewing a long-established pair's bond, cementing the union between new mates and preparing each pair for the nesting cycle soon to follow. Courtship displays include short, quick dives (hunting displays); exaggerated preening and stretching which shows off their magnificent plumage and ritual bill dipping in and out of the water. Then they race off together across the lake with their powerful wings flailing the water. After a circuit of the lake, they return to the starting place. All the while they have been filling the air with their wonderful, musical calls. This courtship ritual has been documented by many fine ornithologists including P. L. Hatch in 1892: "This race was repeated over and over again, with unabated zest, until by some undiscoverable signal it ceased as suddenly as it began."

Nesting

The loon's nest —or platform—is built at the very edge of fresh water lakes or rivers in a quiet, secluded location. Sometimes it is on the shore; sometimes the top of a musk-rat lodge is used to make it harder for predators to reach the nest. The site is built up with reeds, sticks, grasses and muddy vegetation dredged up from the bottom of the lake bed. It is formed into the shape of a mound; roughly one and a half feet in diameter with a slight hollow in the middle.

Wildlife artist Richard Van Order of Boulder Junction, Wisconsin, captured loon mates nesting on the shore of a northern lake. Note the proximity of the nest to the water. *Photo of drawing: Tom Hollatz.*

Both the male and female cooperate in nest building. This part of the breeding cycle is completed by mid May.

Egg-laying begins at this time and can continue as late

as the latter half of June. Mating occurs on the land or, like many waterfowl, on the water. Though the average clutch size is two, one to three eggs are typical. The eggs, sized 2.2 to 3.5 inches long, vary in color from olive through greenish to dull brown with faint black spots. The incubation period, which lasts some 29 days, is a critical time for the loons. Full development of the embryos demands parent attendance and warmth 95 percent of the time. Both parents share incubation duty. Clearly, disturbances from predators or man during this time can easily cause failure and abandonment of eggs. Yet loons will defend their nests by drawing predators away with noisy calling and flapping and outright attacks with their pointed dagger-like beaks. But with their legs placed so far back on their bodies to give them a wonderful advantage on water, they are slow and awkward on land. Often, the only thing a parent loon can do is slip into the water and leave. Many eggs, except the most secluded, are lost.

Loon pair. In the background is the kind of lake shore favored by loons as nesting sites. *Photo courtesy of the Sigurd Olson Institute.*

18

Top: A Common Loon on a nest hidden among reeds adjacent to the shore of a northern lake. *Photo courtesy of the Sigurd Olson Institute.*
Bottom: Eggs of the four species of loons. Upper left: Common Loon. Approx size 3″ Upper right: Arctic Loon, approx size 2¼″. Lower left: Yellow Billed Loon. approx. size 3″. Lower right: Red Throated Loon. approx size 2¼″. *Photo credit: Field Museum, Chicago, IL.*

19

Top: Loon chick on the nest. *Photo: Sigurd Olson and U.S. Bureau of Sports Fisheries & Wildlife.* Bottom: Loon with chick on the water. *Photo: Minnesota DNR.*

Parenting

The chicks' down is a fluffy, dusky brown and is warm and water tight. From hatching, the chicks are good swimmers and by ten to thirteen days of age are skilled in submerging and diving. Loons are devoted parents caring for their young during the first two months after hatching. And as the chicks have a lot of growing to do in the brief northern summers, both parents are kept busy hunting to provide for them. But hunting in these cold northern lakes is what a loon was designed to do. They are superb divers. Going as deep as 200 feet, they catch fish (preferably in the 4 to 6 inch or 10 to 15 centimeter size range), crustaceans and supplement this protein-rich diet with some water plants. When a loon dives for its prey, its dagger-like beak is brought into play with a snake-like thrust of its neck. Securely grasped in its powerful bill, the fish is brought to the surface flipped up into position and caught deftly. The loon has no way to tear at its prey, so it is eaten or fed to its chicks in whole form, usually head first. Yet chicks can manage fish which seem to be nearly as large as themselves. On this rich diet, they grow quickly.

After loons have survived the difficult and critical incubation period and have their precious, dusky chicks hatched and swimming they are better able to defend them. In the wild the chicks are vulnerable to the large, fierce muskie, turtles, other big fish and eagles. Loons will often carry their chicks on their backs, thus preventing such predation. This back-riding also warms the chicks and parent birds will raise their wings slightly to provide wind protection. In areas where such loon family groups draw human attention boaters have been startled by charging, screaming parent birds striking the water with their powerful wings. Loons that have been separated from their chicks by boats have been known to perform these frightening displays while one of the pair dives under and surfaces near the chick. Loons have even completed attacks to the point of using their beaks and drawn blood from intruding onlookers. Their investment in their chicks is great and worth such staunch defenses. But constant defense of this kind is costly for the loon. On populated lakes, where intrusion is a daily occurrence, loons can be in a chronic state of stress. This is not conducive to good parenting and certainly takes much time away from hunting and providing for the chicks. Chick survival is often lowered by human intrusion.

Migration

As the short northern summer comes to an end, and the bright rich colors of fall begin to clothe the land, it is time for the loon to retrace its flight path to the warmer coastal waters of Altantic and Pacific coasts and the Gulf of Mexico. They migrate in small flocks or sometimes attach themselves to skeins of Canada geese. It is not unusual for the adult loons to leave the summer range before the newly flighted juveniles.

The winter fishing grounds provide ample food for the loons. It is believed that young birds stay on the winter range for several years, growing and fattening themselves, before they are sexually mature and are drawn to the cold northern lakes to mate and breed. It is also a time to develop their hunting skills so that when they become parents, they are capable of providing for their young. And as loons are long lived, there is time for young birds to develop these skills on the winter ranges before sexual maturity. On the winter fishing grounds neither the adult birds which migrate north each summer to breed nor the younger growing juveniles not yet sexually mature utter any of the cries which, up north, have made the loon such an interesting bird. On the winter range, the loon is essentially silent.

Other loons—in brief

Yellow-billed loon. *Gavia adamsii* 33-38 inches (83-95 cm). Similar to the Common Loon but with a pale ivory bill. It is almost straw-like, distinctly upturned; straight above; slightly angled below. This is the largest of the loons. In winter its head is darker than the Common Loon and the white spots on the back are larger and fewer. The calls are similar, however.

Range: Arctic; north of the tree limit; from U.S.S.R. to northwest Canada. Winters along Pacific coast of northern Eurasia, southeast Alaska and British Columbia. The range of the Yellow-billed loon overlaps that of the Common loon, north and west of Hudson Bay. It is accidental on the Atlantic coast.

Red-throated loon *Gavia stellata* 25 inches (63 cm). The sharp thin bill, distinctly upturned, is the key field mark. In summer it has a gray head; plain back and rufous throat, while in winter it is marked similarly to the Common loon but is smaller, similar to the merganser in size. Its profile is more snake-like than the Common loon. Unlike the Common loon, however, the Red-throated loon is usually silent, although it has a falsetto wail, falling in pitch or a series of duck-like quacks.

Range: Arctic, circumpolar on both fresh and salt water. It winters along the coasts of the Mediterranean, China and northwestern Mexico.

Arctic or Pacific loon *Gavia arctica* 26 inches (65 cm). The Arctic loon is smaller than the Common loon with a thin, straight bill. In the summer it is marked with squarish white spots on the back arranged in four distinct patches, two on each side. The crown and nape are pale gray. In the winter it is very like the Common loon but grayer and lighter. The back is gray with pale feather edgings, giving a scaly effect.

Range: Rare in eastern U.S. Nearly circumpolar. Winters along the coasts to the Mediterranean, India, and northwestern Mexico.

Photo: Tom Hollatz.

24

The Lord did well when he put
the loon and his music in the world.
                    Aldo Leopold

The Loon
in Song

There is no sound on earth like the eery, haunting song of the loon. It evokes a feeling of primeval wildness in some, vague forboding in others, but no one who hears the calling of a loon is left unmoved. Each time is a wonderful new experience. Often the loon is heard by those already primed for escape from city streets and mundane noise, having traveled to pristine northern lakes; but to those who have heard the loon's call in flight over suburban lots or as a rare visitor on developed lakes, it is just as marvelous, just as exciting. It is the loon's call that really makes the bird. Without its music, the loon is but a beautiful water bird, no more interesting than a merganzer or a goose. It is the call of the loon that singles it out as something special and quite, quite unique.

The loon has a versatile repertoire of calls, each with its own message. There are, however, four basic cries which the loon uses alone or in combination. These are the wail, the tremolo, the yodel and the hoot.

25

The Wail

The wail is a general message call when the loon wants to interact. It can be used between separated parents and their chicks or between a mated pair that have been off on their own hunting. Three types of wail calls have been identified by careful listeners. Type one is a simple single pitch call. Type two starts the same and then jumps to a higher note. It can end on the high note or drop back to the first note. The type three wail starts out following the type two pattern with a lower note followed by a higher one but then the call has an added third note which is higher still. Often the call ends on the lower note again.

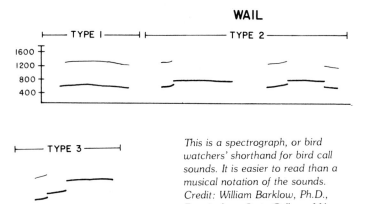

This is a spectrograph, or bird watchers' shorthand for bird call sounds. It is easier to read than a musical notation of the sounds. Credit: William Barklow, Ph.D., Framingham State College, MA.

The Tremolo

The tremolo is indicative of fear or uneasiness in a loon. It is used when the bird has been disturbed or startled by predators or man getting too close or when the chicks are in some danger. It is also the only call the loon uses in flight so that many people who have not heard the other calls have perhaps heard this one as a loon passes overhead. The sound of the tremolo call can rise and fall rapidly. As in the case of the wail, the tremolo has three types. The first is a single modulated note, the second begins with the same pitch and then jumps one-third of an octave higher, and the third is like type two with another step jump up in pitch.

TREMOLO

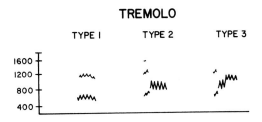

The Yodel

The yodel is the most complex of all the calls. It is used usually when there is aggression between males. Much yodeling can be heard in the spring and early summer when male loons are settling territorial disputes. The entrance of another male into one's territory can set off wild yodeling. During the mating rituals the pair also yodel. The yodel consists of an introduction and then a phrase which is repeated over and over. There can be up to nine repeated phrases in a yodel, with the number directly related to the degree of agitation in the bird. Each loon has its own unique version of the yodel which has led observers to believe this call is used by the birds as an identification call. Indeed, recorded yodels have been used by ornithologists to identify individual birds from year to year.

YODEL

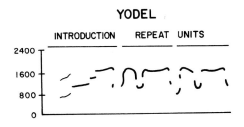

27

The Hoot

The hoot is the simplest of the calls. It is a quiet single note that the birds use to maintain contact in family groups. Loons often change the pitch of the hoot also as in the other calls.

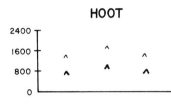

HOOT

The Tremolo-wail

The wail, tremolo, yodel and hoot are the four basic calls. Loons often combine these calls, however. This has led observers to believe that mixed emotions are being conveyed. The tremolo-wail call, for example, which is a cry beginning with the tremolo and ending in the wail could indicate a bird wanting to interact with another but for some reason—as an inexperienced male in another's territory—is afraid or unsure of its own actions. This combined call can sometimes be heard by parent birds when they are trying to reach chicks but are separated by a boat or some other fearful situation.

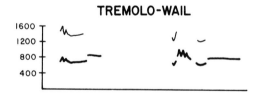

TREMOLO-WAIL

The Tremolo-yodel

This combined call begins with the tremolo, denoting fear or hesitation, and ends in the more aggressive yodel. Border spats often provoke this particular call when the individual bird is confronted by a more aggressive neighboring male or a pair. The resident male is put in a less advantageous position causing the tremolo—expression of fear—and then the territorial mechanism is elicited—the yodel.

TREMOLO-YODEL

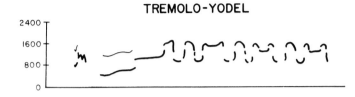

Loons often are compelled to answer the calls of other loons, creating at times incredibly beautiful and strangely haunting concerts. When the silence is broken by a lone loon giving a series of wails or yodels, other loons further out on the lake or even on neighboring lakes join in the chorus creating an intricate melody of sound that can travel through many miles of wilderness, sometimes a whole lake region. "One wail triggers other birds," explained William Barklow, an expert on the study of loon communication. "Every loon on a lake will call at the same time. On a quiet and windless night, the birds on neighboring lakes can hear the chorus and may also begin to call." Loons are sometimes joined by wolves (or vise versa) and it produces a song rich in the wild spirit of the north woods. It is surprising how similar the songs of the loons and wolves really are and how well the two fit together.

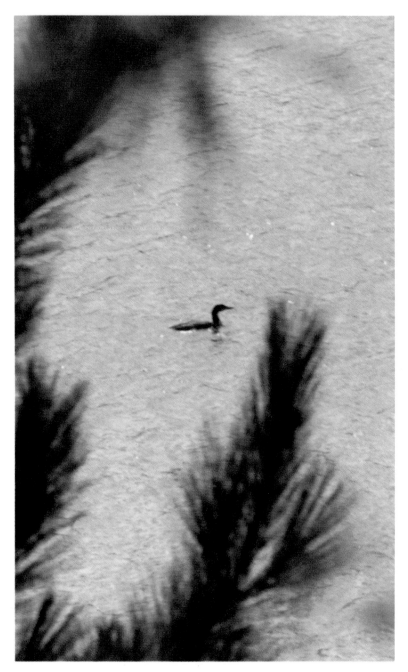

Photo: Tom Hollatz.

The Loon in Legend

The wonderful and haunting music of the loon has created an aura of mystery around the factual bird such that, for many people past and present, the loon embodies more than song and bright feathers. It is the stuff of omen, of dreams, of legend.

To many of the native American peoples, the loon is a revered personage much more than mere bird. The Cree Indians respected the loon as "Mookwa" or "Spirit of Northern Waters." They believed that the loon's call was the cry of a dead warrior forbidden entry into heaven. Ojibwa (Chippewa) Indians revered the loon as "Mang" or "The most handsome of birds." They heard the haunting cry of the loon as an omen of death.

Gathered here are several of the most common stories and legends in which loons have a role. The first and likely the most familiar of these is the wonderful story of how the loon acquired its speckled back.

The Loon's Necklace

—A Tsimshian Indian Legend

An old man who was recently blind lived with his wife and young son near a salmon stream. Because it was winter and he could no longer hunt, the old man and his family were starving. One morning the wife went searching for dried berries, leaving the boy to care for his father. The unhappy old man set remembering when he was a great hunter and feeling miserable that he no longer could provide for his family.

Suddenly, the youth spotted a bear on the other side of the stream and had an idea.

Taking his father's hand, he took him to the edge of the stream. There he put a bow and arrow in his hands. He said, "I'm going to help you kill a bear,"

"How can I aim?" his father replied.

"I will be your eyes," the boy said.

Standing on a rock, the boy pointed the arrow at the bear's heart.

"Shoot!" he cried. The old man pulled hard and the arrow sailed through the air. It hit the bear's heart, killing it instantly and it toppled over dead.

Before the boy could tell his father that the bear was dead, an old hag appeared. She lived alone near their clearing and was feared for her magical powers. She had been watching the old man and the boy as they killed the bear and thought of all the meals it would give her. The bear had enough meat to last her through the rest of the long winter.

"Good for you, old man," she chortled. "You hit a log." The hag then called to the boy, "Come with me," and stepped into his canoe.

Afraid, the boy got in and they crossed the stream. The hag threatened the boy, telling him that if he told his father that he killed a bear she would give him a beating "or worse."

33

The hag and the boy skinned the bear and then made a fire to cook some meat. She sat muttering to herself as she stuffed her mouth with the tasty meat. "Why should the old man have any food. He is blind and useless anyway." She was so occupied with cooking and eating her meat that she failed to see that the boy hid some pieces of meat in his clothing.

When he got back to the clearing and the old woman had disappeared with a portion of the meat, the boy told his father that he had killed the bear.

"The old woman said she would beat me if I told you," the boy said.

"Here, father, I saved you this piece of meat."

His father would not touch it. He was ashamed that his son should have to steal to feed him. "Keep it for your mother," he told the boy.

Then he stood, resolved, and reached for the boy's arm. "Take me to the lake," he told his son. "I will visit Loon there. Loon is a wise and magical bird who might help me."

At the shore, the old man said, "Now leave me."

The boy replied, "Let me stay with you, father."

"Go," his father said, "Mother will return soon."

Alone, the aged man sang about being miserable and helpless. "Ha-no ha-no hi-hi-ye-ee!" he chanted over and over again. He then cried, "My heart is breaking with grief."

After many hours, another song reached his ears. The song was sad and lonely. The old man soon smiled because he knew it was the song of Loon. Again, he heard the song. This time it was louder and closer. Then again it came, closer and louder from just off shore.

"You sing of troubles," Loon said. "How can I help you?"

The old man replied, "O Loon, I am old and blind. My family is starving and I can't feed them. I do not ask to be young, but I would not be so helpless if I could see. I would

35

give my most priceless possession to see again."

Loon said, "Enter the water with me. Hang onto my wings as I dive and bury your eyes in my feathers."

The old man did so. Hanging onto Loon's wings, both of them dived down, down and deeper down. Then they floated toward the surface.

Just as he thought his lungs would burst, the old man and Loon reached the surface. Loon asked, "Can you see?"

"Just a little." He rubbed his eyes. "I can see the shape of some trees."

Loon said, "Dive with me again."

Again the old man held onto Loon's back and buried his face in his feathers. They dove, deeper this time and for so long a time that the old man was sure he would die. But they broke the surface of the cold water just as he was passing out. He gasped the air in deep gulps.

Suddenly, the old man cried, "I can see! I can see!"

Indeed, his sight had been restored. The old man pulled a shell necklace from his neck and tossed it over to Loon. It fell on Loon's neck, while a sprinkling of loose shells scattered over his back. Where the white shells touched the black feathers, white markings appeared. Loon preened itself admiringly and swam quietly away.

The old man returned to his clearing, rejoicing in his returned vision. It began to rain just as he reached his lodge. His wife had returned and was consoling their son who was crying.

Between sobs, the boy told him, "The old woman beat me. She found out that I gave you some of the meat."

Comforting his son, the old man said, "Forget about the beating. I am now able to see. We will not want for meat anymore and the old woman will hit you no more."

It began to rain very hard. Lightning flashed repeatedly and thunder deafened them. The old man and the wife blocked the entrance to their lodge to keep it dry inside. Between claps of thunder, they heard the old hag outside their door. She was trying to get inside out of the storm. The old man would not answer her or open the door. For some time she pounded on the door and screamed at them but they would not let her in.

The following day the clearing was washed clean and the old hag was gone. But the old man saw an owl which he had never seen before. That night the owl screamed all night keeping them awake. It was the same the next three nights so that the family finally had to move to a new clearing. They were sure that the old hag had turned herself into the owl just to annoy them.

With the old man's returned vision, they were not hungry again. Every time they heard Loon call from far out on the lake, they were grateful. And it seemed that Loon's cry was no longer always sad. Often they heard Loon's long, happy thrill.

"Loon is laughing," the old man explained. "Loon is pleased with his new necklace."

In this tale the loon is a bird of magical powers. One gets the feeling that it is a most powerful and wise personage capable of much more than restoring the sight to an old man.

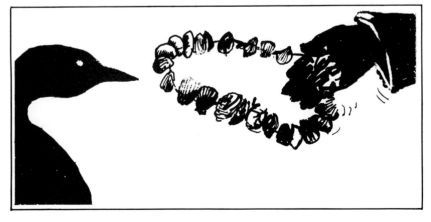

The Loon Woman

Once, long ago there lived a loon woman. Because she was not really human but half supernatural as well, she was shunned by many people and feared for her magical powers. This made her life very lonely. One day near a lake, she found a strand of hair. As she fingered the supple strength of the strand and studied its color and texture, this lonely loon woman began to long for the person to whom it belonged. She began to search for the owner of the single strand of hair. After a long time she finds the man whose hair it is but discovers also that he is her brother. So enamored is she of the man that she is willing to transgress the incest taboos to have him and begged him to go away with her. But the brother would not ignore the taboos and escaped her, returning to his family. This put family at great risk for the loon woman is violently enraged by his escape. She began to search for them, but they hide. Finally, not to be outdone, the loon woman set the forest on fire. It is so great a fire that there can be no escape. A wise man of the family has them enter a sky basket that can carry them up over the fire to safety. They are cautioned, however, that looking down at the fire would break the spell and all would perish. They agreed and are carried up over the great flames of the fire only to fall to their destruction when one of them breaks the taboo of looking down. They burned and their hearts burst from their bodies as pure white coals. The loon woman gathered the coals together, stringing them about her neck. It is said that only when the family is revenged by the death of the loon woman can the white coals be brought back to life by the gods. The loon wears its white-spotted back still.

Here the loon was a symbol of power as in the first legend, but there is a much more sinister overtone to the whole tale and a link between the loon and death, or more precisely, the world in between death and life.

The Creation Legend

The loon also figured into some versions of the creation legend of which there are too many variations to list. However, most versions involve people, either human or half-gods, stranded on the back of the huge sea turtle. The endless sea on which the turtle swims is either the primeval ocean before land is made or the result of the classical flood. In most variations, the loon is hailed from flight and asked to dive down to find some soil from which dry land can be made. The loon dives and is down a long time but returns without soil. He dives again and is gone even longer only to have his lifeless body float to the surface. A muskrat is then hailed as it swims by and is also asked to dive down to gather a bit of ocean bottom to make a new world. The muskrat agrees to try and dives. On the first try, like the loon, the muskrat is unsuccessful and so dives again. On the second dive, his lifeless body floats to the surface after a long time. But a bit of earth is in its paws. From this soil grows all the dry land of today. The lifeless bodies of the loon and the muskrat are molded anew into the life forms of birds and animals to populate the new world with man.

This legend sees the loon in a far more natural light than previous legends. It is significant, however, that it is the loon, of all birds, which makes the attempt, thus pointing to the esteem the Indians held for the bird.

How Language Was Lost

In this legend Kuloskap is a god-like folk lore hero of the Passamaquoddy Indians of Maine.

Kuloskap had given mankind many things. He had taught him how to make and use a bow and arrow, he had showed him what plants and animals were to be used for food, he had schooled man in the laws of hunting and had given man happiness. He was therefore grieved when he saw man being greedy with food, unjust with his laws or cruel to each other. He decided that he would go away.

He made one last great feast for all his creatures and man, which could speak to each other through a common language. The feast was wonderful. It was then Kuloskap told them all that he was going away.

Kusloskap got into his canoe at the end of the evening to sail away across the lake. All the animals and birds and man stood by to watch. The canoe slipped into the water and drifted out into the lake. Dusk and mist soon hid the canoe from sight but for a long time all could hear the great Kuloskap singing from out on the water.

All the creatures of the earth had silently watched and listened as Kuloskap drifted away. When the last faint notes of his song were gone, one by one they turned from the lake. It was then they discovered that they could no longer speak to one another. They were sure it was because Kuloskap had left them. After noisily trying to make sense of the jabberings of each tongue, they gave up and left the place of the feast to lead each his own life. Loon, however, resolved to try to call Kuloskap back so that a common language could be restored to them. Loon called and called to the great Kuloskap but he did not answer.

Loon calls still, in the quiet of misty evenings and in the hush of cool dawns. Loon still hopes for a unity between all creatures by bringing Kuloskap back.

How the Loon Got Its Song

A great warrior of near-god stature wanted a messenger he could send between the worlds of gods and men. He called to the loon on the lake and asked him if he would act as this messenger.

"But how will I call for you?" asked the loon.

"I will give you a song to sing so that I will know it is you who calls and not my enemy," said the great warrior.

The loon agreed and the warrior taught the loon his song as he sings it now.

But as it happened, soon after this the great warrior became displeased with the people he had created on the earth and he chose to leave them. The loon called after the great warrior trying to convince him to return. He calls still.

Again the loon is an intermediary between the world of gods and the world of men.

Drawing by Jeff Ayers.

Ah, if I could put into the word that music which I hear, that music which can bring tears to the eyes of marble statues! . . . to which the very muscles of men are obedient!   Henry David Thoreau Sept. 23, 1852

The Loon
in Literature

It is not surprising that the loon has found its way into literature. From Thoreau to the present, loons have provided the inspiration for prosaic and poetic passages. It is easy to romanticize about loons. Their vivid plummage, their wonderful, musical song, even their secretive, shy habit are easily the fodder for fertile minds. Here is gathered a sampler of writing about and inspired by the loon.

Henry David Thoreau on "The Loon"

In the fall the loon came, as usual, to molt and bathe in the pond, making the woods ring with his wild laughter before I had risen.

As I was paddling along the north shore one very calm October afternoon, for such days especially they settle on to the lakes, like the milkweed down, having looked in vain over the pond for a loon, suddenly one, sailing out from the shore toward the middle a few rods in front of me, set up his wild laugh and betrayed himself. I pursued with a paddle and he dived, but when he came up I was nearer than before. He dived again, but I miscalculated the direction he would take, and we were 50 rods apart when he came to the surface this time, for I had helped to widen the interval; and again he laughed long and loud, and with more reason than before. He maneuvered so cunningly that I could not get within half a dozen rods of him. Each time, when he came to the surface, running his head this way and that, he coolly surveyed the water and the land, and apparently chose his course so that he might come up where there was the widest expanse of water and at the greatest distance from the boat. It was surprising how quickly he made up his mind and put his resolve into action. He led me at once to the widest part of the pond, and could not be driven from it. While he was thinking one thing in his brain, I was endeavoring to divine his thought in mine. It was a pretty game, played on the smooth surface of a pond, a man against a loon. Suddenly your adversary's checker disappears beneath the board, and the problem is to place yours nearest to where he will appear again. Sometimes he would come up unexpectedly on the opposite side of me, having apparently passed directly under the boat. So long-winded was he and so unweariable, that when he had swum farthest he would immediately plunge again, nevertheless; and then no wit could divine where in the deep pond, beneath the smooth surface, he might be speeding his way like a fish, for he had time and ability to visit the bottom of the pond in its deepest part. It is said that loons have been caught in the New York lakes 80 feet beneath the surface, with hooks set for trout—though Walden is deeper than that. How surprised must the fishes be to see this ungainly visitor from another sphere speeding his way to their schools! Yet he appeared to know his course as surely under water as on the surface, and swam much faster there. Once or twice I saw a ripple where he approached the surface, just put his head out to reconnoitre, and instantly dived again. I found that it was as well for me to rest on my oars and

46

wait his reappearing as to endeavor to calculate where he would rise, for again and again, when I was straining my eyes over the surface one way, I would suddenly be startled by his unearthly laugh behind me. But why, after displaying so much cunning, did he invariably betray himself the moment he came up by that loud laugh? Did not his white breast enough betray him? He was indeed a silly loon, I thought. I could commonly hear the splash of the water when he came up, and so also detected him. But after an hour he seemed as fresh as ever, dived as willingly and swam yet farther than at first. It was surprising to see how serenely he sailed off with unruffled breast when he came to the surface, doing all the work with his webbed feet beneath. His usual note was this demoniac laughter,

Photo credit: Minnesota Department of Natural Resources.

yet somewhat like that of a water-fowl; but occasionally, when he had balked me most successfully and come up a long way off, he uttered a long-drawn unearthly howl, probably more like that of a wolf than any bird; as when a beast puts his muzzle to the ground and deliberately howls. This was his looning—perhaps the wildest sound that is ever heard here, making the woods ring far and wide. I concluded that he laughed in derision of my efforts, confident of his own resources. Though the sky was by this time overcast, the pond was so smooth that I could see where he broke the surface when I did not hear him. His white breast, the stillness of the air, and the smoothness of the water were all against him. At length, having come 50 rods off, he uttered one of those prolonged howls, as if calling on the god of the loons to aid him, and immediately there came a wind from the east and rippled the surface, and filled the whole air with misty rain, and I was impressed as it were the prayer of the loon answered and his god was angry with me; and so I left him disappearing far away on the tumultuous surface.

Gus Anderson's "Our Loon"

Lusty loon of the lake,
laughing and lurking—
grabbing nature's essence
screaming out loud into
silent night.

Lovers echoing your tremolo
on quiet island on
White Birch Lake,
trobbing hearts,
throbbing wails.

J. Parker Huber on Loons

Dressed in summer in a black cap with a white neck scarf and piebald cape, they move almost invisibly across dark waters. Sometimes these solitary hunters swim with only their bills exposed, like submarine periscopes scanning their surroundings.

From *The Wildest Country: A Guide to Thoreau's Maine*

Sigurd F. Olson on the Loon

Above came a swift of wings, and as the loons saw us they called wildly in alarm, and took the laughing with them into the gathering dusk. The shores echoed and re-echoed until they seemed to throb with music. This was the sound that more than any other typifies the rocks and waters of forests and wilderness.

Hamlin Garland: "The Loon"

At some far time, this water sprite
A brother to the coyote must have been,
For when the sun is set,
Forth from the failing light
His harsh cries fret
The silence of the night,
And the hid wolf answers
With a wailing keen.

From "Prairie Song and Western Story" (1898)

Edward Howe Forbush on the Loon

Of all the wild creatures which still persist in the land, despite settlement and civilization, the loon seems to best typify the untamed savagery of the wilderness. Its wolf-like cry is the wildest sound now heard in Massachusetts, where nature has long been subdued by the rifle, ax, and plow. Sometimes at sea, when I have heard the call of the loon from afar, and seen its white breast flash from the crest of a distant wave, I have imagined it the signal and call for help of some strong swimmer, battling with the waves....

From *Game Birds*

Tom Hollatz: The Call of the Loon

In the gathering dusk,
Hear the loon's wild cry.
Is he laughing or crying?
Nature's clown is full of love
Moving with grace on northern waters.
Diving, playing games with silent onlooker,
Thoreau in awe of checker-board moves.
Olson thrilling to echoing cries off
Rocks and waters of forests and wilderness.
Loon-laughing bursts of melancholy,
Painting velvet night walls in wild hues.

Kathleen White, excerpt from "Loon"

You could never know the power you possess—
    drawn by your pulse—quickening calls,
    I've come to catch a glimpse of you.

I've listened to your mournful cries;
    your mystic, recluse laughter filled my nights
    with ecstatic contentment.
Sunrise brought a yearning to see you.

Paddling the canoe alone is a strange sensation;
I don't like the clatter
    as the raised bow slaps every ripple.
I sit awkwardly in the middle,
    paddling slowly, quietly, ineptly,
    not wishing to disturb or startle you in any way.

I sense your nearness—
    even your silence draws me closer,
    increasing my excitement and anticipation.

Movement near shore attracts my gaze,
    quickens my breathing.
A gray form swims out of the shadows into full view,
    a familiar shape;
    black-and-white markings become distinguishable.

Breathing itself seems risky
   as I try sculling the water to get closer.
   A glimpse will not suffice!

You've lifted my soul to unbelievable heights
   I sit in utter amazement
      watching you glide toward me.
   You are beautiful.
   Do you know I love you?

Top: Loon and chick. *Photo: Tom Hollatz.* Bottom: Loon eggs. *Photo: James LaVigne.*

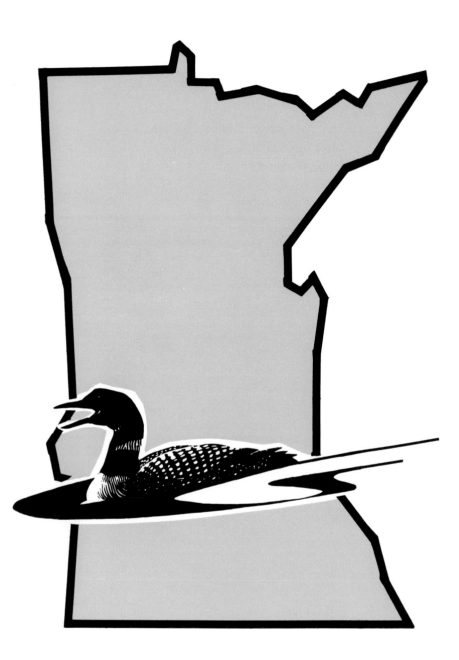

The Loon in Symbol

Minnesota's State Bird

Loons evoke emotion. Those who have stood at the edge of a cold northern lake and listened to the melodious music of a loon at dawn know a deep love of the loon. But even for those who have never heard the call, never seen the real bird dive on a lake or fly, musically, overhead, there is still a deep affection for the bird. It is not surprising, therefore, that Minnesota, which has the largest population of loons in the adjacent 48 states should select the loon as its state bird.

In 1949 Minnesota's legislature appointed a state bird commission to select from eight candidates: the pileated woodpecker, wood duck, belted kingfisher, killdeer, scarlet tanager, rose-breasted grosbeak, mourning dove and the common loon. The commission included ornithologists, museum directors and state officials. Their first task was to set up criteria for the selection. They are as follows:

Photo: James LaVigne.

1. Since this is to be a distinctive trademark or insignia for the state, it should be a bird which no other state has as State Bird.
2. It should be fairly well known, though not necessarily abundant.
3. It should occur throughout the state at least during the nesting season and preferably during the entire year.
4. It should be a strikingly marked bird whose pattern, even in black and white, would lend itself well to use in insignia.
5. It should have a special significance for Minnesota.

Voting for the best of the eight choices included school children, sportsmen's clubs, other organizations and interested citizens. At that time, however, the voting was inconclusive. There was no agreement between the different groups. The legislature found opinion so split that they took no action.

The Minnesota Ornithologists' Union continued to press for the common loon. After several years of effort, they were able to bring public opinion and the legislature around to their view. In 1961, the legislature passed bills making the common loon the official state bird in place of the American goldfinch. Minnesota, the state of 10,000 lakes, seems a fitting state to have a state bird which is part of those lakes and part of the north country.

"Loon" drawn by Jason Barr

Opposite: The third graders at the Arbor Vitae-Woodruff Elementary School in Woodruff, Wisconsin, are learning about the Common Loon. From left to right are Meagan Ryan, Chadd Bartlett and Jerry Kriewald. The teacher is Mary Herrick. *Photo by Tom Hollatz.*

The Loon
in the Hearts of . . .

. . . Children

It is surprising how well the loon is known by even very young children. They love the loon, and in the examples that follow, draw the loon very, very well. These wonderful sketches are from third graders at the Arbor Vitae-Woodruff Elementary School in Woodruff, Wisconsin.

Top, opposite: Jerry Kriewald drew a happy loon near a northern shoreline.
Bottom, opposite: Meagan Ryan showed a Common Loon enjoying dinner.
Above: Erin Neuberger, age 9, drew this picture of a loon.

... Artists

But one does not have to be a child to enjoy the loon in art. Indeed, there are many who enjoy using the loon as subject matter for their creative talents. Here are some examples of loons portrayed in stained glass, sculpture, and on canvas.

Above: This magnificent stained-glass window showing two Common Loons was created by Charles F. Betz III of Los Angeles. The art piece now hangs in Joe Kelly's Landing in Woodruff, Wisconsin. *Photo: Tom Hollatz.*
Top, opposite: Howard "Pop" Dean of the St. Germain and Sayner, Wisconsin area spends his time carving loons as well as other creations. *Photo: Tom Hollatz.*
Bottom, opposite: A beautiful loon painting by Robert Metropulos, 1983.

. . . Towns

Yes, towns! Mercer, Wisconsin, proclaims itself the "Loon Capital of the World." In honor of their proclamation and to make people aware of the protective habitat of the loon, a colossal statue of the Common Loon was erected next to the town's information center. The fiberglass statue weighs 2,000 pounds and stands a whopping 16 feet tall.

"Loon Capital of the World," Mercer, Wisconsin, displays this huge loon for visitors. *Photo: Tom Hollatz.*

... Shopkeepers

The popularity of the loon has made loon "things" good business, especially in those areas of the north woods where loons are actually found. The volume of these loon treasures is enormous: books, statues, pictures, stuffed toys, records, ash trays, pins, stickers . . . the list of loon-facetted merchandise is endless. And people love it all.

Above: The loon is "in" as a collectible and the variety of items with loons on them or created in the shape of loons is quite amazing. *Photo: Tom Hollatz.*

Print courtesy of Richard Van Order of Boulder Junction, Wisconsin.

Wilderness can be appreciated only by contrast, and solitude under-stood only when we have been without it.   Sigurd F. Olson

The Loon in the Wild ... and Man

Can the loon survive? This is a very important question. The loon can be popular and loved and officially protected, and still not survive. Indeed, the very fact that it is popular can contribute to its decline. The loon is a wilderness bird unable to withstand constant invasion into its private life. And whether this invasion is harassment by curious boaters eager for a look at nests or by civilization making inroads into isolated areas, the loon still suffers. Every year lakes which enjoyed the music of loons in previous seasons are silent. Nesting areas become lawns. Hunting grounds become water ski runs. Every year the loons having success in rearing their chicks are those pairs nesting further and further north.

In the 1920s, loons were commonly sighted north of a line from New England to northern Iowa. Earlier ornithologists indicated that loons once lived even further south. Today loons are found only in upper reaches of Michigan, Wisconsin and Minnesota along with scattered pockets in the northern areas of the upper New England states.

There have been loses by natural disasters: In 1963-1964 alone, almost 7,000 loons perished along the shores of Lake Michigan, victims of botulism. Mortality estimates for the fall migration prepared in late October and early November, 1963, were 3,240 loons; 2,260 gulls; 50 ducks; and 10 grebes. In 1976, 600 loons were found dead along the southern and southeastern shores of Lake Michigan. Loons have been injured or killed landing on ice-glazed roads, probably mistaking them for rivers.

Another potentially disastrous factor is the longevity of the loon. Since loons are thought to be very long lived (perhaps 20 to 25 years), it is difficult to determine just how stable the loon population really is. If the current population is composed of old birds, a population "crash" could occur. For this reason it is vital that the number of chicks successfully reared each year remains sufficient to preclude such a disastrous event. Biologists are concerned. And because the loon is so secretive with nesting, studies of the loon population and habitat use must constantly be upgraded.

Research and Breeding Surveys

In 1982, something wonderful happened concerning a new awareness of loons. The spark was provided by "On Golden Pond." Playing a vital role in that filmmaking was the North American Loon Fund of Meredith, New Hampshire, whose affiliate provided technical assistance. That unit also protected nesting loons during the filming. The loon calls in the movie came from the album "Voices of the Loon," published by the North American Loon Fund in association with the National Audubon Society.

The North American Loon Fund (NALF) is a vehicle for people all across the continent who care about loons to offer support to these organizations and research projects. The following reports were collected and shared by the NALF.

Jane Arbuckle, wildlife director of the Maine Audubon Society, reports on the Maine Common Loon Project:

". . . Regions and/or lakes in southern Maine that were organized early in the summer conducted loon counts during the last week in July, with counts taken by all watchers in a given area at 7:00 a.m. and/or 7:00 p.m. on the same day. From 111 lakes within organized regions, 337 adult loons (83 pairs) and 76 chicks were seen on morning counts, and 302 adults (93 pairs) with 81 chicks were seen in the evenings. An additional 10 lakes outside organized regions reported 51 adult loons and 16 chicks."

Carroll Henderson, director of the Minnesota Department of Natural Resources, reports on the Minnesota Loon Observation Program:

". . . the most remarkable discovery of 1982 was a loon nest containing four eggs, twice the usual number. Loon banding was quite successful in 1982, with 40 loons—including 31 chicks and nine adults—captured and banded, bringing to about 100 the total number of loons banded by the department during the last three years."

Breeding status of the Common Loon in Montana as reported by P. D. Skaar, project director at Montana State University:

"First-hand observations of loons were made during a four-day (July 13-16) search of 234 lakes, revealed 154 loons on 59 lakes, with some 50 pairs producing 31 chicks."

Project Loon Watch, Oikos Research Foundation, Judith McIntyre, director, reports:

"The Oikos Project Loon Watch involves the volunteer monitoring of lakes in Minnesota and New York. More than 1,000 volunteers have participated since Minnesota's program began in 1970 and New York in 1977. . .

"Results to date show that Minnesota's loon population and reproduction have remained stable since the early 1970s with 72-85 percent of all pairs having successful hatches. . ."

Adirondack Loon Preservation Project, the Adirondack Council, George D. Davis, project director, states:

". . . Historical research revealed over 1,000 lakes and ponds throughout northern New York state potentially suitable for loon nesting. Reliable reports of recent loon sightings were found for 192 of these lakes, and loon nesting has been reported since 1970 on 126.

"The project also began gathering historical data of loon breeding success that will provide the basis for future research on the effects of acid rain on loon reproduction."

Breeding status of the Common Loon in Vermont was indicated by Sarah B. Laughlin, director of the Vermont Institute of Natural Science:

". . . Fewer adult loons were observed in Vermont in 1982 (42 compared to 56 in 1981), but an equal number of territorial pairs (24) and more attempted nesting (19 versus 1981's 15) were counted. Only 12 nesting attempts (62%) were successful, producing 14 chicks."

Wisconsin Project Loon Watch shared this from the Sigurd Olson Environmental Institute, Jim Pierce, coordinator:

"In 1982, the fifth field season for Wisconsin Project Loon Watch, volunteers covered 494 lakes and identified

1,086 adult loons, including 389 pairs; they sighted 380 chicks of which 234 survived through fall migration. Total loon population is estimated at 1,500 to 2,000 birds.

"Based on five years of observation on a sample of 35 lakes, it appears that the state's population is stable or increasing. . ."

From New Hampshire Loon Recovery Program, Loon Preservation Committee of the Audubon Society of New Hampshire, Jeffrey S. Fair, director:

"The loons of New Hampshire's lakes enjoyed their most successful year in 1982 since statewide survey and recovery efforts were organized in 1976.

"This year's population survey covered about 150 lakes and ponds over a 10-week period from mid-May through July. Record high numbers were reported of adult loons (257), loon pairs (104), chicks hatched (91), and surviving chicks (76). The total population tally grew from last year's high of 308 to 338 this year, largely due to a one-third increase in chick productivity and the continued success of artificial nesting islands, which produced one-fifth of the chicks.

"After a half-century of decline in New Hampshire, during which half of the loon breeding lakes were abandoned, the loon population appears to be leveling off. It is hoped that the two-year gain . . . may presage a recovery in this state."

And from James A. Sherburne, leader of the Maine Cooperative Wildlife Loon Research, University of Maine:

"Traditional nesting sites for loon population on four lakes in northern Maine were monitored. From 17 territorial pairs (11 nesting pairs), 19 eggs were laid, 12 eggs hatched, and seven chicks fledged. . ."

Free Ride. *Photo by Woody Hagge, 1981.*

The Wisconsin Department of Natural Resources also is conducting experiments with four-by-four floating platforms which could be used by breeding loons as a nesting area. In theory, the mechanics of a floating platform would seem to protect loon eggs from waves or sudden increases in lake levels. An island would adjust to whatever water conditions and kept away from all but the most determined predators. Anchored in lakes in remote parts of the north, it would provide a safe haven for loon eggs. But according to Ron Eckstein, Wisconsin DNR wildlife manager, "People, seeing the platforms, aim their boats at them just to take a look at the nesting loons."

Ontario Lakes Loon Survey of the Long Point Observatory, David Hussell and Robert Alvo, project directors had this information on acid rain:

"The potentially devastating effect of acid rain on loon reproduction was the focus of much of 1982's research. . ."

"Eighty-four lakes in the vicinity of Sudbury, Ontario, were visited from June 12 to July 18; 81 were visited from July 31 to August 21. Lakes were searched for the presence of loons and nests, and were sampled and tested for acidity and other relevant characteristics.

"The survey revealed that lakes with high acidity had a significantly smaller chance of supporting breeding loons than did lakes with less acidity, strongly suggesting that acid precipitation is adversely affecting the breeding success of Common loons in parts of Ontario."

Peek-a-Boo. *Photo by Woody Hagge, 1981*

The populations of loons, as reported by these states, seems to be stable or slowly increasing. This is good. But the human use of many of the same lakes where loons nest is gradually increasing also. Harmony must be maintained or the loon will loose ground again. Caution must be observed around loons at all times, especially during the nesting period, to insure stable loon numbers. Posters and

warning signs by the loon project affiliates help. Education helps. The love of the loon is there, understanding of the loon, in all its needs and requirements to survive, must follow.

Everyone can help

Not everyone is fortunate enough to live on a lake with loons and daily hear their musical calls. The ability to occasionally visit loon-inhabited lakes is even a privileged experience not afforded to all. But the love of the loon is more widespread than the number of people able to exprience the loon first hand. For all those people who have affection for this black and white diving bird and wish to help, even in a small way, there are avenues ready made. The North American Loon Fund is open to all to share in the preservation of the loon. Some 30 states now have a non-game check box on their state income tax returns. This fund exclusively benefits such wildlife as the loon, bald eagle and

An example of the signs posted at lakes inhabited by loons.

Wisconsin's Project Loonwatch posts this sign to caution the curious to steer clear of loon.

endangered species not aided by the sale of hunting licenses. States which do not have this clause on the state tax returns might include them if citizens let their legislators know they are interested.

When around loons

For those fortunate enough to have access to lakes where loons frequent or nest, special help can be given in the effort to preserve this marvelous bird. Both Minnesota and Wisconsin have posters which they set up on lakes inhabited by loons. Citizens living on such lakes can see to it that signs are posted and then follow the cautions listed on them. The cautions are as follows:

1. Steer clear of loons on the water—definitely do not chase them with boats.

2. Do not separate members of loon families—this causes great stress for the birds.

3. Avoid shoreline areas used by loons as nesting sites—this is very important as the loon is so sensitive to intrusion at the nest site.

It is important to remember that the loon is a protected species making harassment illegal and punishable. It might be fun to chase loons and make them dive but it is also against the law. Everyone who shares lakes with loons must respect these wonderful birds and allow them the wildness they need to survive.

Photo courtesy of the Minnesota Department of Natural Resources.

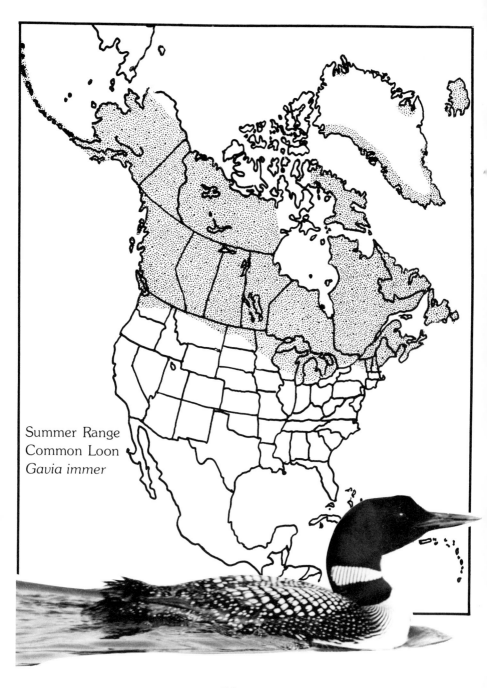

Summer Range
Common Loon
Gavia immer

Do not go gentle into that good night.
Rage, rage, against the dying of the light.   *Dylan Thomas*

Appendix

The following is a list of organizations dedicated to the study and preservation of the loon. Information about each organization can be obtained from the addresses shown.

Loon Project
Adirondack Council
P.O. Box D2
Elizabethtown, NY 12932

Wisconsin Project Loon Watch
Sigurd Olson Environmental Institute
Northland College
Ashland, WI 54806

Minnesota Loon Appreciation Committee
812 Oriole Lane
Chaska, MN 55318

Loon Survey Project
Vermont Institute of Natural Science
Woodstock, VT 05091

Common Loon Protection Project
Maine Audubon Society
118 Old Route 1
Falmouth, ME 04105

Loon Preservation Committee
Audubon Society of New Hampshire
Main Street
Meredith, NH 03253

Ontario Lakes Loon Survey
Long Point Bird Observatory
P.O. Box 160
Port Rowan, Ontario
N0E 1M0

Wisconsin Project Loon Watch is asking for your help. If you live or vacation in the northwoods, you can volunteer to help monitor a lake. If you do not, you still can help by making a tax-deductible contribution to Wisconsin Project Loon Watch. You gift will help maintain research and education efforts on behalf of the loon. The Common Loon has been labeled a "watch species," according to Jim Pierce of Wisconsin Project Loon Watch. We must help keep the northern lakes a safe haven for this magnificent bird.

Those wishing to help, please contact:

Wisconsin Project Loon Watch
Sigurd Olson Environmental Institute
Northland College
Ashland, WI 54806
715-682-4531   ext. 489

The Authors

Tom Hollatz is an outdoor writer and resort owner/operator in Boulder Junction, Wisconsin. He currently writes columns for several outdoor magazines and has also written several books. He is a former managing editor of the Chicago *Daily Calumet* newspaper and was a copy and photo editor at the Chicago *Tribune* for 12½ years. Tom and his wife Cassie reside in Bear Lodge at Boulder Junction.

Corinne Dwyer was born in Massachusetts but grew up in several states. A graduate of the College of St. Benedict, St. Joseph, Minnesota, with a B.A. in Biology, she has maintained a strong interest in nature coupled with artistic and writing talents. She has been a veterinary assistant and a college lab instructor. In addition to currently working as a paste-up artist for a typographic firm, she operates a kennel of champion fox terriers and airedales on her small Minnesota farm.

Other Titles by North Star Press

The White Earth Snowshoe Guide Book *Tom Hollatz*
All aspects of snowshoeing are dealt with. An excellent book for the novice and expert alike. **paperback $3.50**

Ducks of the Mississippi Flyway *John McKane, illustrated by Ken Haag and Ernest Strubbe*
The artists capture the ducks in natural settings, and the paintings add spark to the text. **paperback $2.98**

A Catfish in the Bodoni *Otto J. Boutin*
Great fun to read, either for pure entertainment or for its glimpses into a vanishing phenomenon—the tramp printer. **cloth $4.00**

The Wizard of the Winds *Ward T. Van Orman*
The world champion balloonist, Ward Van Orman's chronicle of his balloon racing adventures. Unique. **cloth $12.00**

The American Buffalo in Transition *John A. Rorabacher*
What is of genuine value in this extensively illustrated book is the text devoted to the buffalo today. **cloth $6.50**

A White Pine Empire *John E. Nelligan*
A skillfully selected sheaf of intensely interesting and supremely amusing reminiscences of a logger's life told in the plain, simple language of the lumberman. **cloth $7.50**

Gazehounds & Coursing *M. H. "Dutch" Salmon*
An illustrated guide to the art and sport of hunting with sight hounds, featuring breeds and training. **cloth $18.50**

We Went A Loggin' *Esther Gibbs*
A delightfully droll and true to life tale of a post-World War I couple who try to make a go of life as settlers in the cut-over timber lands of northern Wisconsin. **paperback $3.00, cloth $4.95**